When the Lights Came On

Four complete children's Christmas programs for schools and churches

Phyllis Vos Wezeman & Anna L. Liechty

Standard
PUBLISHING

CINCINNATI, OHIO

Dedication

With appreciation to Gloria Yancey,
     who shares God's message through the gift of music. P.V.W.

With grateful memories to Bev and Elizabeth Brown,
     who helped make the costumes, find the music, and oversee
     the rehearsals of many a Christmas production. A.L.L.

Scripture taken from the HOLY BIBLE, NEW INTERNATIONAL
VERSION®. NIV®. Copyright© 1973, 1978, 1984 by International Bible
Society. Used by permission of Zondervan Publishing House. All rights
reserved.

Standard Publishing, Cincinnati, Ohio
A division of Standex International Corporation
© 2002 by Phyllis Vos Wezeman and Anna L. Liechty

ISBN 0-7847-1392-8

TABLE OF CONTENTS

INTRODUCTION

When the Lights Came On contains four complete programs for use in church and school settings. Each separate script centers on the theme that Christmas is a celebration of God's message of love and hope for the world; however, the plays also include the theme that each of us who receives God's message is challenged to share God's good news with others.

Angels: Heralds of Hope is a traditional retelling of the angels' involvement in the Christmas story, emphasizing God's message of hope for the world. *Carols Come to Life* conveys the story of Jesus' birth through the music of the season, the stories behind those songs, and their significance for today. *Prints of Peace* is a play in which a family's "wish list" provides an opportunity to learn that God's gift of peace is meant to be shared. *The Menagerie at the Manger* invites us to experience God's message using all of our senses.

Each script can be easily adapted to include a cast of few or many participants ranging in age from preschool children to youth and adults. The programs can be staged simply or elaborately in the sanctuary or in a social hall. Lighting and sound would enhance any production; however, the message is not dependent upon special effects or scenery. The addition of props and costumes may be embellished as time and resources permit, or leaders may use the suggestions provided to communicate the basic context for each pageant.

Each program contains four parts. There is an introduction to the play with a statement of theme, a summary paragraph, and production notes, including: cast/personnel, costumes, music, props/equipment, and set/staging. Also included are Advent preparation suggestions to actively involve participants in anticipating and enhancing the production. A bulletin/program outline is listed; however, it must be adapted to include additional or alternate music selections as well as the names of the participants. A complete script, which may be duplicated as needed, is provided.

No matter which program is selected, the meaning is the same: God's gift of Jesus at Christmastime is a message we all need to hear again and again, reminding us that we must be the light in a dark world and bring the good news to a waiting world.

ANGELS: HERALDS OF HOPE

THEME: God's messengers, the angels, bring hope to the world with their cry, "Good news! God is with you!"

SUMMARY: Designed to be presented within a worship setting, this traditional retelling of the angels' involvement with the Christmas story features five tableaus highlighting interactions between God's messengers and the Biblical participants. Narrators tell the story of the angels' appearance to explain each tableau. Scripture and song serve as connectors and transitions between the scenarios. In the first two story scenes, the angel Gabriel amazes Zechariah with the promised hope of answered prayer and then hails Mary's acceptance of God's plan for salvation in the birth of a Messiah. Next, an angel in a dream calms Joseph's doubts with words of assurance. Then the angel appears to the shepherds and announces that hope is born to all people of peace. That angel is joined by a heavenly chorus of angels affirming in glad adoration God's realization of hope in the world.

SUGGESTIONS: "Angels: Heralds of Hope" is a program, staged in a worship setting, that can be presented simply or elaborately with many or few participants. Scripture and Story Scene readings should be assigned to older youth or adults, while children of any age may share in the music and the tableaus. Each of the five segments requires participants to read the Scripture passage, to provide the narration for the Story Scene, to enact the tableau, and to perform the music. Readings may be further broken down to allow for more than one participant per section. For example, the Scripture could be shared responsively between two readers or verses may be assigned to members of a class. The script for the commentary on the Story Scene could have different people reading each paragraph. For the concluding commentary, "The Angels' Message to Us" lines may be read by the five previous narrators, or by a sixth speaker, or the words could be used as a responsive reading between a leader and the congregation. One reader per section, or another person, should be designated to light the four Advent candles, as well as the Christ candle in the center of the wreath, at the conclusion of each commentary. In summary, parts should be adjusted to accommodate any number of participants, but could include: Accompanist; Candlelighters (5); Class, Choir, Instrumental, or Solo Musicians; Scripture Readers (5); Story Scene Narrators (5 or 6); Angel Gabriel (two scenes); Angel to Joseph; Angel to Shepherds; Angel Chorus; Joseph; Mary; Shepherds; Zechariah; Worship Leader(s).

Tableaus are still scenes portrayed in costume in which the players assume a dramatic pose and hold their positions while a narrator interprets the represented event. Again, these may range from minimal to lavish in their staging. The scenes should take place where they can be seen from all parts of the congregation. The participants may simply strike a pose in the center of the stage area or on a raised platform, or the scene may be highlighted with a special "frame" to focus attention on the tableau. Actors should be costumed appropriately to suggest their parts, adding props that help project the image of each character.

Music may range from instrumental or vocal solo performances to class, choir, group, or congregational singing. Additional or alternate carols may be substituted for those suggested.

Advent activities involving the creation of "angel" banners or illustrations are suggested as a way to prepare the children for Jesus' birth and for the Christmas service.

ANGELS: HERALDS OF HOPE ADVENT ACTIVITIES

Advent is a season of preparation for the coming of Christ, occurring the four Sundays prior to Christmas Day. During Advent, the church prepares for the birth of Jesus as a babe in a manger, and for the rebirth of Christ's presence in the hearts of faithful people. To help children learn about the meaning of Advent, as well as prepare for Christmas, use an Advent wreath and light one candle each week in the classroom or worship setting. During the program, "Angels: Heralds of Hope," the white center candle, representing Christ, will be lit and used to ignite the candles of the congregation.

As a visual for the program, create five angel banners for display in the sanctuary or hallway. Highlight the words used to describe the theme of the angels' messages: Amazement, Acceptance, Assurance, Announcement, and Affirmation. Choose purple or blue fabric for the backgrounds. Add angels cut from white silk or satin and bond to fusible web. Iron the pieces onto the background. Glue on any details or trims. Letter one of the words on the top, bottom, or side of each banner. To hang the pieces, add a rod and cord to the top of each banner. For a simpler project, create the banners from paper and have the children illustrate each story scene. Another option would be to design a bulletin board or bulletin covers featuring the children's interpretation of the angel appearances.

As one way to practice music for the program, feature an angel carol or hymn each week of Advent and share them during the Christmas worship service.

ANGELS: HERALDS OF HOPE Bulletin/Program Format

PRELUDE: "Angels, from the Realms of Glory"
CALL TO WORSHIP

CAROL: "O Come, All Ye Faithful"
INVOCATION

The Angel of Amazement—Luke 1:13-17
Story Scene—Tableau of the Angel Gabriel and Zechariah
Music: "O Come, O Come, Emmanuel"

The Angel of Acceptance—Luke 1:30-33; 35
Story Scene—Tableau of the Angel Gabriel and Mary
Music: "We'll Call Him Jesus"

The Angel of Assurance—Matthew 1:20, 21
Story Scene—Tableau of the Angel and Joseph
Music: "Joseph Dearest, Joseph Mine"

The Angel of Announcement—Luke 2:10-12
Story Scene—Tableau of one Angel and Shepherds
Music: "The First Noel"

The Angels of Affirmation—Luke 2:14
Story Scene—Tableau of Angel Chorus with Angel and Shepherds
Music: "Angels We Have Heard on High"

THE OFFERING

MUSIC: "While Shepherds Watched Their Flocks"

The Angels' Message to Us *(Responsive Reading)*

Sharing the Message of Hope

CAROL: "Silent Night! Holy Night!"

BENEDICTION

POSTLUDE: "Hark! the Herald Angels Sing"

ANGELS: HERALDS OF HOPE (Script)

PRELUDE: "Angels, from the Realms of Glory"

CALL TO WORSHIP: God's messengers bring us hope in the midst of life's problems: "Do not fear! God is with you!" Listen for these angelic words today as we worship and celebrate the birth of hope—the birth of Christ.

CAROL: "O Come, All Ye Faithful"

INVOCATION: O God of hope, inspire us with the message of this day. Help us to sense the presence of the heavenly host as we join them to celebrate the good news of Jesus' birth. O God, bless us as we worship that we may hear the angels' message and make room in our hearts for the Savior You sent. Amen.

THE ANGEL OF AMAZEMENT

Scripture: Luke 1:13-17

Story Scene: Stage tableau of the Angel Gabriel and Zechariah.

Narrator: The Angel Gabriel's words amazed Zechariah. We can feel sympathetic with his amazement. Probably we, too, would have trouble believing a message such as this even if we stood in the very presence of one of God's angels. For his unbelief, Zechariah was unable to speak until God's promised hope had been fulfilled: John was born to Elizabeth and Zechariah in their old age.

Although Zechariah had not ceased to pray for a child, he was astounded when the prayer was answered. Perhaps that is like us today. We pray, but don't really expect God to answer. The first message of the angels is that God hears our prayers and sends answers that bless not only us, but all of God's people.

As the people of God we should prepare to be amazed. God will do what God promises. That is our hope. God doesn't promise just to fulfill our wish list, but to fulfill our deepest longings. The first message of the Christmas angels is to prepare to be amazed. Nothing is too hard for God. Even in the face of the impossible, we have the promise of hope. *(Light the first Advent candle.)*

MUSIC: "O Come, O Come, Emmanuel"

(Angel Gabriel and Zechariah leave at the conclusion of the music.)

THE ANGEL OF ACCEPTANCE

SCRIPTURE: Luke 1:30-33, 35

STORY SCENE: Stage tableau of the Angel Gabriel and Mary.

NARRATOR: Gabriel's message to Mary, like the message to Zechariah, was astounding, a seemingly impossible promise. Unlike Zechariah, however, Mary did not doubt that God could accomplish such a miracle. She only wondered how God would bring a baby to her when she was yet unmarried. From the first moment of the news, Mary's attitude was one of acceptance. This time it was Gabriel who was amazed that such a trusting human being existed.

Life brings surprises to us all. God's people can learn from Mary's pattern to recognize God's surprises and to respond in gentle acceptance. "Nothing is impossible with God," Gabriel told Mary. And so, in faith, Mary's first thought was to go to her cousin Elizabeth to rejoice with her over God's hope conceived within each of them.

When, like Mary, we offer our complete acceptance of God's plan for our lives, we, too, discover the hope that begins to live and grow within us. Then we can become a channel for God's blessing of hope to be shared in the lives of other people. The coming of Christmas challenges us to offer a gift to God—the gift of our acceptance of the Holy Spirit within our lives. And then hope is conceived anew. *(Light the second Advent candle.)*

MUSIC: "We'll Call Him Jesus" (Karen Dean. *Sing a Song of Scripture.* Kansas City, MO: Lillenas, 1986.)

(Angel Gabriel and Mary leave at the conclusion of the music.)

THE ANGEL OF ASSURANCE

SCRIPTURE: Matthew 1:20, 21

STORY SCENE: Stage tableau of the Angel and Joseph.

NARRATOR: God's surprising promise of hope does not come without changing our lives. And, like all human beings, Joseph struggled with how to respond to the changes in his life. This time the angel comes with God's message in the midst of fitful sleep, reassuring Joseph that the Holy Spirit not only brought about these circumstances, but would be with the couple throughout their experience together. Joseph found that he could face whatever life brought, so long as he had God's assurance of hope.

Joseph was faced with what choices to make in response to change, just as we often are today. Sometimes we agonize so much over what to do that we block out the assurance God keeps offering. As God's people, we must learn to listen for the message of reassurance in whatever way God presents it—even whispered to us in our sleep.

The Christmas angels herald a hope that is backed by God's own guarantee—if we are open to the leading of the Holy Spirit we can be sure that God's hope will not fail us. Changing circumstances are all around us, but so is God's message of a hope we can count on: promised to us, conceived within us, and guaranteed with God's own presence. *(Light the third Advent candle.)*

MUSIC: "Joseph Dearest, Joseph Mine" *(Composer B. Cabena)*

(Angel and Joseph leave at the conclusion of the music.)

THE ANGEL OF ANNOUNCEMENT

SCRIPTURE: Luke 2:10-12

STORY SCENE: Stage tableau of one Angel and Shepherds.

NARRATOR: Have you ever felt like you were waiting for something to happen, but you didn't quite know what it was? The shepherds were "abiding" in the field—just waiting, stargazing, perhaps—responding to that inner human sense that the universe revolves on hope. On the first Christmas Day, the shepherds were the first to hear the messenger from God proclaim that the long hoped-for promise of God was this day a reality! A Savior was born!

The shepherds hadn't prayed for a child to be born as had Zechariah; none of them had been proclaimed a "favored one" attuned to God as had Mary; they probably weren't wrestling with any deep matters of conscience as had Joseph. They were simply there, nearby, in the quiet of the hillside, available to hear the good news. But they heard the angel's voice.

This Christmas Day we are here, gathered in the quiet, available to hear the message of good news that the angel brings to us: today is the baby born, today is the great joy, today is God's Christ coming to all who will hear the message and respond with hearts tuned to God's peace. For us, as for the shepherds, hope is not just some future possibility. Hope is born today! *(Light the fourth Advent candle.)*

MUSIC: "The First Noel"

(Characters in tableau remain in place at the conclusion of the carol.)

THE ANGELS OF AFFIRMATION

Scripture: Luke 2:14

Story Scene: Add Angel Chorus to tableau with Angel and Shepherds.

Narrator: Suddenly there they were. Can you imagine the heavenly host all together at once praising God and affirming to the shepherds the glory of what they had heard? One angel is mind-boggling, but an angel chorus must have been awe-inspiring. No wonder the shepherds wanted immediately to "go and see" this hope born to all people.

  The story of the birth of Christ, the Hope of the World, was affirmed that night to the shepherds. And still two thousand years later, the story is one that is told and retold around the world. But it isn't enough just to hear the story—to hear "about" the hope God sent in Jesus Christ. We must share the story, affirm its power with others who also have been touched by hope. It is in joining together that we experience anew the mystery of the Christmas message.

  And so we gather today in affirmation. God's hope is here among us, within us, surrounding us, and binding us together as one glorious multitude of believers who celebrate that because of this day—because of this Christ child—the world is forever changed, our lives are forever founded on hope. We can live confidently, at peace with one another, because we have heard the angels' affirmation: Good news! Great joy! Fear not! Hope is ours! *(Light the Christ candle.)*

MUSIC: "Angels We Have Heard on High"

(Angels and Shepherds leave at the conclusion of the music.)

THE OFFERING *(Receive an offering for a special cause or mission project. Place a wooden manger at the front of the sanctuary and invite worshipers to come place their gifts, symbolic of offering themselves to the Christ Child.)*

MUSIC: "While Shepherds Watched Their Flocks"

THE ANGELS' MESSAGE TO US

(Stage a tableau by having each character reenter as his or her name is mentioned. If desired, Mary could carry a baby or a doll in this scene.)

ONE: Angel messengers brought hope to people of Bible times and their messages still bring us hope today.

ALL: These themes still echo through the stories that we share.

ONE: Zechariah renews our amazement at God's power to answer our prayers.

ALL: Mary teaches us acceptance of God's will for our lives.

ONE: Joseph offers us assurance that our fears and doubts can be overcome.

ALL: The Shepherds confirm God's announcement of peace for all people.

ONE: The Angels' "Alleluias" empower us to join in the affirmation of Christ's birth.

ALL: Now we leave to share Christ's message with others, and then we, too, become God's Heralds of Hope.

SHARING THE MESSAGE OF HOPE

CAROL: "Silent Night! Holy Night!"

(As the carol begins, the worship leader lights a candle from the Christ candle, and in turn lights the candles of the ushers, who then take the light to the first person in each pew. Each person, in turn, "passes the light" to his neighbor.)

BENEDICTION: Just as the light from one candle kindles enough light for us all, so the light of Christ brings hope to the world through our lives. Take Christ, the Light of the World, as your confidence; take Christ, the Joy of the World, as your companion; take Christ, the Savior of the World, as your hope. Go in peace. Be God's messengers of hope.

POSTLUDE: "Hark! the Herald Angels Sing"

CAROLS COME TO LIFE

THEME: Christmas carols and the stories behind them help us share God's message of love for the world.

SUMMARY: "Carols Come to Life" retells the story of Jesus' birth in a pageant that connects music of the season, the stories behind the songs, and their significance for today. Three scenes, which are set in home, church, and community, share the music and its message as interpreted by a Narrator playing the role of a Christmas Caroler. In Scene 1, a family gathered for Advent devotions makes clear the theme of waiting as the Narrator shares the story behind the carol "O Come, O Come, Emmanuel." Scene 2 takes place in church as a children's choir practices for the Christmas Eve service and learns the message behind the words to "O Little Town of Bethlehem." In the third vignette a live nativity scene forms in front of a community shelter and the Narrator connects the message of "O Come, All Ye Faithful" to the timeless truth of Christmas. Finally, the spiritual "Go, Tell It on the Mountain" challenges participants to share the good news of Christ's birth with the world.

SUGGESTIONS: "Carols Come to Life" is a program, staged in a pageant or a worship setting, that can be presented simply or elaborately with many or few participants. Guidelines are offered for Cast/Personnel, Costumes, Music, Props/Equipment, and Set/Staging.

CAST/PERSONNEL: It is suggested that children of different ages and grades, as well as older youth and adults, have specific parts in the preparation and the presentation of this program. Adjust the number of people in each scene to fit the number available or desirable for the pageant. For example, in Scene 1 the carolers could be prekindergarten through grade one children, while the caroler/narrator, father and mother should be older youth or adults. Although parts are provided for a daughter and a son in the kitchen table scenario, additional children may be added to the family scene. In Scene 2, the children's choir might include boys and girls from grades two, three, and four. Individual speaking parts may be added by creating parts for more than the three children listed in the script. Roles of the children's choir accompanist and director, as well as the caroler/narrator, should be played by older youth or adults. For Scene 3, the live nativity could be comprised of students in grades five and six and include as many angels, shepherds, and wise men as needed to involve everyone in the production. Adults or older youth should play the Caroler/Narrator, Joseph, Mary, and the Stranger. If additional speaking roles are desired, there could be more than one Caroler/Narrator in each of the three scenes. Suggested parts include:

Scene 1: Carolers, Daughter, Father, Mother, Narrator, Son
Scene 2: Accompanist, Child One, Child Two, Child Three, Children's Choir, Choir Director (Miss Brooks), Narrator
Scene 3: Accompanist, Children's Choir and Choir Director from Scene 2, Angels, Carolers from Scene 1, Family from Scene 1, Joseph, Mary, Narrator, Shepherds, Stranger, Wise Men
Personnel: Accompanist, Lighting Technician, Music Director, Pageant Director, Props/Stage Manager, Sound Coordinator

COSTUMES: Participants should be costumed to help project the image of each character.
Accompanist—contemporary clothing
Angels—garland or halos, white robes
Carolers—coats *(optional)*, gloves/mittens, hats, scarves
Children's Choir—choir robes or stoles
Choir Director—contemporary clothing
Family (Daughter, Father, Mother, Son)—contemporary clothing
Joseph—head covering, robe
Mary—head covering, blue and white robe
Narrator (Caroler)—coat *(optional),* hat, scarf
Shepherds—head covering, robes
Stranger—contemporary clothing
Wise men—crowns, gifts, robes

MUSIC: Five Christmas carols are integral to the story and should be used in the program. They include:"O Come, O Come, Emmanuel" "Go, Tell It on the Mountain"; "O Come, All Ye Faithful"; "O Little Town of Bethlehem"; "Silent Night! Holy Night!" As an option, incorporate additional songs by children's choirs, congregation, instrumentalists, or soloists at the beginning or end of the pageant and between scenes.

PROPS:
Scene 1: Advent wreath, Bible, candles, chairs (4), kitchen window, matches, table
Scene 2: Chairs, church window, hymnals, music, music stands, piano, shaker jar with Bethlehem snow scene, whistle
Scene 3: Bales of hay, manger, storefront window

EQUIPMENT: Keyboard, organ or piano; lighting equipment; microphones; sound system

SET/STAGING: To perform this script in a traditional format on a stage, create three distinct settings on the stage. Downstage left, set up the "home" for Scene 1 with a kitchen window to define the area. Add a table and four chairs. Place an Advent wreath and a Bible in the center of the table. Downstage right, set up the "choir room" location with a church window to define the space. To create the scene, use chairs or pews that face center stage and a director's music stand. Hymnals and sheet music stacked around the area will help to create the picture of controlled chaos. Position Scene 3, the "City of Hope Shelter," upstage center. A painted storefront window serves as a backdrop. Bales of hay and a manger are brought in later and placed in front of the "window" to create a traditional nativity scene. For ideas on constructing the windows for the home, church, and community locations, refer to the suggestions under "Advent Activities."

ADDITIONAL INFORMATION: Additional Advent activities are suggested as a way to prepare the participants for Jesus' birth as well as for the Christmas pageant. An outline for a printed bulletin or program is offered, however, it must be adapted to include additional or alternate music selections, as well as the names of the participants. In addition, indicate where the audience is to participate and to stand. A complete script is also provided. It may be duplicated and distributed to those with speaking parts.

CAROLS COME TO LIFE—ADVENT ACTIVITIES

In preparation for the pageant, "Carols Come to Life," as well as for the celebration of Christ's birth, use any or all of the suggested activities.

CREATE SHAKER JARS

Make shaker jars similar to the one used in Scene 2's Children's Choir rehearsal scenario.

MATERIALS: Electrical tape; glitter; illustration of Bethlehem; mineral oil or baby oil; plastic lids; scissors; silicone rubber sealer or other water-proof glue; small jars with lids (baby food size); waterproof permanent markers.

METHOD: Cut a silhouette of the town of Bethlehem from a plastic lid. Be sure the shape fits inside of the jar lid. Use permanent markers to add color and detail to the design. Place a mound of silicone glue in the center of the inside of the lid. Set the "town of Bethlehem" in the middle of the glue and allow it to dry.

  Place about one-fourth teaspoon of glitter in the jar, then fill it almost full with mineral or baby oil. Spread some silicone glue around the inside lip of the lid and screw the cover on the jar tightly. If desired, reinforce the seam with electrical tape.

HOLD A FAMILY ADVENT FESTIVAL

Celebrate Advent with an event to help the entire Sunday school, even the entire congregation, prepare to explore and experience Jesus' birth. Use this unique design—Gather! Explore! Celebrate! Share!—during one or more church school sessions, as a special children's or intergenerational program, or as a community outreach opportunity. In keeping with the theme, "Carols Come to Life," highlight this emphasis for various portions of the event.

GATHER! Gather the participants in the sanctuary for music and an explanation of the program. Sing Advent hymns and Christmas carols. Besides congregational singing, music may be presented by choirs, soloists, small groups, and instrumentalists.

EXPLORE! Continue the event in a large room, such as a social hall, or in individual classrooms, where a variety of learning activities have been prepared in advance.

CELEBRATE! At the conclusion of the activity time, form a procession, and journey from the social hall to the sanctuary for a time of worship including carols, Scripture, prayer and a brief devotion.

SHARE! Following worship, invite the participants to the social hall to share refreshments or a meal.

LEARN HYMN STORIES

In addition to learning the music for the five songs highlighted in the "Carols Come to Life" pageant, use children's stories and object lessons to invite all ages to hear the message of faith behind the words they sing. These are located in the following resources:

"Go Tell It on the Mountain," Wezeman, Phyllis Vos and Anna L. Liechty. *Hymn Stories for Children: The Christmas Season.* Grand Rapids, MI: Kregel Publications, 1997.

"O Come, All Ye Faithful," "O Come, O Come, Emmanuel," and "O Little Town of Bethlehem" Wezeman, Phyllis Vos and Anna L. Liechty. *Hymn Stories for Children: Special Days and Holidays.* Grand Rapids, MI: Kregel Publications, 1994.

"Silent Night! Holy Night!," Wezeman, Phyllis Vos and Anna L. Liechty. *Hymn Stories for Children: The Apostles' Creed.* Grand Rapids, MI: Kregel Publications, 1995.

MAKE THE SCENERY

In the weeks ahead of the Christmas program, involve youth in creating scenery to suggest the three locations in the pageant: home, church, and community. One simple technique is to construct cardboard or pine frames for windows. For Scene 1, create a square kitchen window; for Scene 2, form an arched church window; and for Scene 3, make a large, rectangular storefront window. The first two windows must be simple frames, open so that the audience can see what is going on behind or to the side of them. Cut the outer shapes from cardboard and add thinner strips as "panes." Paint the frames appropriately. The storefront window forms a backdrop for a live nativity scene, and so the "window" can just be painted on cardboard or cloth with the words "City of Hope Shelter" or other messages that suggest the setting. Depending upon the area used for staging these scenes, the windows may be hung, suspended from the ceiling or a framework. The windows may also be positioned on the floor with a supporting brace.

CAROLS COME TO LIFE Bulletin/Program Format

GATHERING MUSIC: Christmas carols

WELCOME

OPENING PRAYER

SCENE 1: Scene 1 takes place around the kitchen table of a family home as parents and children prepare for Advent devotions.

CAST *(List in order of appearance)*

CAROL: "O Come, O Come, Emmanuel"

SCENE 2: Scene 2 is set in the rehearsal space of a church as the Children's Choir practices for the annual Christmas program.

CAST *(List in order of appearance)*

CAROL: "Silent Night! Holy Night!" *(Verse 1)*

SCENE 3: Scene 3 occurs in front of the "City of Hope Shelter" as participants prepare to stage a live nativity scene.

CAST *(List in order of appearance)*

CAROL: "O Come, All Ye Faithful" *(Verse 1)*

CLOSING CAROL: "Go, Tell It on the Mountain" *(Refrain)*

CAROLS COME TO LIFE (Script)

Scene 1

Parents and children sit around a kitchen table with an Advent wreath in the center ready for family devotions. The father prepares to read Scripture. A Narrator, dressed as a caroler, introduces the scene.

NARRATOR *(enters thumbing through a book of Christmas music, humming or singing the first lines of several songs; he looks up and notices the crowd):* Merry Christmas! How nice to see all of you joining me for a night of caroling! How many "Carols" are with us tonight? Just joking—I was talking about Christmas carols! This is the time of the year for music to really move us! In fact, if we moved through this neighborhood we would see the power that carols bring to our lives in all sorts of ways! Let's just stroll down the street here and do a little "listening in." I wonder how many carols we can hear? It looks like the Smith family is about ready to begin their evening devotions. That's a great time to sing!

(Narrator pauses to listen in at the window of the family kitchen.)

FATHER *(picking up the Bible):* On this first Sunday in Advent, our Scripture passage comes from Isaiah 7, verse 14: "Therefore the Lord himself will give you a sign: The virgin will be with child and will give birth to a son, and will call him Immanuel."

SON: I didn't know they had computers back when Jesus was born.

MOTHER *(looking puzzled):* Son, don't be silly. What makes you think they had computers when Jesus was born?

SON: Well, we have manuals today for our computers. Dad said they were getting a "manual" as a sign from God.

FATHER *(looking perturbed):* That's Im-manuel, Son. It's one of the names of Jesus! It means "God with us."

DAUGHTER: Isn't there a song about "Immanuel"?

MOTHER: Yes, there is a beautiful carol that we sing as we prepare for the time for Jesus to be born.

SON: Then somebody ought to tell folks what it means!

(The Father affectionately ruffles the Son's hair while the Narrator responds. During the Narrator's speech, the family lights the Advent candle and all bow their heads in prayer. They hold this pose throughout the explanation of the carol.)

CAROLER: The boy's right. We sing many carols at Christmas, yet we don't always know what they mean or where they come from. Take the song, "O Come, O Come, Emmanuel," for example. It's been around so long that no one really knows exactly who wrote it, but it has been sung for almost a thousand years! The words were first used at evening prayers as a chant between two groups. The first group sang a verse about one name of Jesus and then the other would sing the next in response. Each line, then, is a prayer for Jesus to come and an opportunity to rejoice at the thought that God will send the promised Messiah who will be Emmanuel—God with us!

(Carolers enter and move toward the Narrator, singing, "O Come, O Come, Emmanuel" as though they were performing for the family who stands at the window and listens appreciatively. The Narrator begins to "direct" each side to sing the "Rejoice! Rejoice!" refrain antiphonally. On the last verse, he also invites the congregation to join in the chorus. As the song ends, the Carolers exit, and the attention shifts back to the family who have been singing with the Carolers.)

SON: Now I know what Immanuel means! But if God sent Jesus to be with us to show us the way—isn't that sort of like a manual? *(Shaking their heads, the family leaves.)*

Scene 2

The Children's Choir at First Church rehearses for the annual Christmas program. The Narrator walks to center stage, quietly singing "Silent Night! Holy Night!" He crosses to the "Choir Room" Scene and stands "outside" the Church talking to the audience.

NARRATOR: It's amazing how quiet and peaceful it can seem when everything is blanketed with snow. Sometimes the world seems just too beautiful for words, and a hush falls over all of creation.

(A group of noisy children enter the Choir Room to rehearse for the annual Christmas program. The children shout and tease each other and make general mayhem until the bedraggled Choir Director, who seems to have laryngitis, blows a whistle to get everyone's attention.)

NARRATOR *(speaks loudly above the crowd of children)*: Well, maybe it's not so quiet and peaceful at First Church where they're trying to practice for the Children's Christmas Program!

CHILD ONE: I'm tired of singing! How many times do we have to practice these songs.

CHILD TWO: Is it time for snacks yet? Do we get snacks? You gave us snacks last week!

CHILD THREE: Has anybody seen my worm? Don't worry, it's a gummy worm. I think Tommy ate it!

CHILD ONE: Are you crying, Miss Brooks?

(Miss Brooks begins to shake a snow scene of Bethlehem.)

CHILD TWO: No, she's just shaking. Why are you shaking, Miss Brooks?

CHILD THREE: Look, it's a snow scene inside a jar!

EVERYONE: Cool!

CHILD ONE: Wow! It looks like snow falling on Bethlehem.

CHILD TWO: Oh, I get it, she wants us to practice "O Little Town of Bethlehem" next!

(The Narrator comes into the scene to help out the poor Choir Director. He takes the snow scene from Miss Brooks and addresses the children.)

NARRATOR: Hey, Everybody! Maybe I can help. Miss Brooks seems to have lost her voice. Maybe before we sing your song, you would like to know a little bit about the story behind "O Little Town of Bethlehem."

CHILDREN *(in unison):* Okay! Sure! Why not!

CHILD TWO: Do we get snacks if we listen?

NARRATOR: What would it be like if we were all sitting on the hillside looking at Bethlehem, just like the night Jesus was born? *(As he speaks, he shakes the snow scene and the children sit down and get quiet, obviously thinking about his question.)* That would be a special scene to try to describe, wouldn't it? Phillips Brooks, the author of "O Little Town of Bethlehem" thought about that question too. He had trouble finding words to share the feelings he experienced when he visited Israel and saw the city where Jesus was born. He wanted to tell everyone in his church about the peace he had felt, just like the peaceful scene inside the shaker jar. He wanted others to recognize the calm, still presence of God as they thought about the first Christmas Eve. So he wrote the words to the song as a poem and asked his organist to write the music. Just the night before the program, the organist finally had the inspiration for the tune we sing today.

Sometimes things seem like they are never going to come together. That's when we need to get quiet and let the peace of

Christmas come into our hearts. I think that you can really sing "O Little Town of Bethlehem" now. Let's try to help everyone experience the place of wonder where Jesus was born!

(Miss Brooks leads the Children's Choir as they sing "O Little Town of Bethlehem." After the carol, the children and Miss Brooks leave quietly, arms around shoulders, at peace with each other and the world as the carol is played one last time. Only the Narrator is left on stage.)

NARRATOR: "And he will be called Wonderful Counselor, Mighty God, Everlasting Father, Prince of Peace" (Isaiah 9:6).

(The Narrator begins to sing "Silent Night! Holy Night!" again as he crosses to the next staging area. He invites the congregation to sing with him, repeating the familiar first verse.)

Scene 3

NARRATOR: I told you music moves us! Whether we're at home or at church or even . . . let's see . . . This is a great place for caroling! It's just like being at the manger of Bethlehem. I've lost track of where I am, however . . .

(As the Narrator speaks, people dressed as Angels, Shepherds, and Wise men bring items and set up an outdoor nativity scene. They greet each other and make decisions about where the props should be placed. A "Stranger" wanders over to observe what's going on and overhears the Narrator's statement.)

STRANGER: You're at the City of Hope Shelter, Buddy. Some guy got the idea to put up a live nativity scene.

NARRATOR: Well, that's a great place for a nativity scene! Mary and Joseph certainly had no place to stay. They were far from home and in need of shelter.

(When the "props" are in place, the Angels, Shepherds, and Wise men leave. Joseph and Mary, carrying a baby, enter and position themselves for the live nativity scene.)

NARRATOR: The story is recorded in Luke 2:6, 7: "While they were there, the time came for the baby to be born, and she gave birth to her first-born, a son. She wrapped him in cloths and placed him in a manger, because there was no room for them in the inn."

STRANGER: I don't think anybody's gonna come to a shelter to see some people standing around in the cold.

NARRATOR: Sometimes it takes time for God's message to get through; or maybe we have to invite people to share God's good news. How about singing, "O Come, All Ye Faithful"? Do you know it?

STRANGER: I sang it as a kid. Didn't everybody?

NARRATOR: Yes, for centuries! That song has been a part of God's message to Christians for countless years. The words have been sung in different languages and to different tunes, but the message is what is important: we are all called to be faithful, to come to the manger.

STRANGER: Well, if we sing, at least we'll stay warm.

(The Narrator and the Stranger begin to sing at the live nativity setting. Slowly others begin to join them as the music continues. On the first refrain, the Angels enter and take their places in the scene. The Carolers and the Family from Scene One enter and move to one side of the set. On the refrain of the second verse, the Shepherds enter and kneel at the manger and the Children's Choir from Scene Two enter and move to the other side of the set. At the beginning of the third refrain, the Wise men enter and take their positions. The Narrator motions for the congregation to join in singing the refrain one more time.)

NARRATOR: God's faithful people have received God's message! We have come to the manger to worship the newborn King. But the story doesn't end there! What we have received must be shared! The rich spirituals of the deep south help us remember that we must put ourselves in the song. We must become God's messengers too. Our challenge is not only to come and be faithful, but also to go and to tell—anyone who will listen—anywhere they may dwell.

(The Narrator moves to center stage and begins to sing "Go, Tell It on the Mountain" slowly and quietly, but picks up the tempo and volume as the music continues. The Stranger joins in, then the Carolers and the Choir, and finally they motion for everyone to sing with them. The Stranger and the Narrator leave singing while characters in the live nativity scene remain in place. A benediction, as well as a curtain call, are optional ways to close the program.)

PRINTS OF PEACE

THEME: Christmas challenges us to share the message that Jesus is God's gift of peace for the world.

SUMMARY: "Prints of Peace" is a play that revolves around a struggle within a family of school-aged children. The children are fighting over Christmas catalogs, magazine ads, newspaper circulars, and internet printouts as they draw up wish lists for their holiday gifts. Their arguments end in "freeze frames" that are interspersed with musical scenes performed by choruses composed of children from various classes or grades. Ultimately, when the catalogs are in "pieces," the youngest child draws a handprint-shaped dove of peace. Grandma then challenges the siblings to draw their Christmas dreams of peace—something they will work to achieve. The family unites behind a goal of enlisting children in their church to "draw dreams of peace." The drawings are featured in the pageant and can be literally displayed in the church or school, as well as the community, after the program is over.

SUGGESTIONS: "Prints Of Peace" is a program, staged in a pageant or a worship setting, that can be presented simply or elaborately with many or few participants. Guidelines are offered for Cast/Personnel, Costumes, Music, Props/Equipment, and Set/Staging.

CAST/PERSONNEL: In this program, the family members—primarily a father, mother, grandmother and three children of various ages, are the principal players. Children from various classes and grades are involved in choruses for various scenes.

Classes/Choirs
Scene 2: Grades Two and Three
Scene 3: Grades Four and Five
Scene 4: Kindergarten and Grade One
Scene 6: Kindergarten through Grade Five

Family: Younger Child, Middle Child, Older Child, Father, Mother, Grandmother

Personnel: Accompanist, Lighting Technician *(optional)*, Music Director *(optional)*, Pageant Director, Props/Stage Manager *(optional)*, Sound Coordinator *(optional)*

COSTUMES: Everyday clothes are appropriate for all characters. Dad and Mom may wear coats when they leave for the mall.

MUSIC: Learn new words to familiar tunes and write additional verses to convey the theme of the program.
Scene 2: "All I Want for Christmas" *(new words)*
Scene 3: "Jingle Bells" *(new words)*
Scene 4: "If You're Happy and You Know It" *(new words)*
Scene 6: "Joy to the World!" *(new words)*

ADDITIONAL MUSIC: Songs that contain the word "peace" can be included in the program as the Prelude, the Postlude, or a time of audience participation at the beginning or the end of the pageant. Selections may include: "Hark! the Herald Angels Sing," "It Came upon the Midnight Clear," and "While Shepherds Watched Their Flocks."

PROPS/EQUIPMENT: Catalogs, chairs and/or sofa, construction or drawing paper, crayons, markers, colored pencils, paints, newspapers, wish list with pictures, keyboard, organ or piano, lighting equipment *(optional)*, microphones, sound system

SET/STAGING: "Prints of Peace" requires two separate staging areas: one for the family vignettes and one for the chorus numbers. Ideally, the family scenes should be played downstage nearest to the audience, with the chorus joining in from behind on a platform or risers.

ADDITIONAL INFORMATION
Advent activities are suggested as a way to prepare the participants for Jesus' birth as well as for the Christmas pageant. An outline for a printed bulletin or program is offered, however, it must be adapted to include additional or alternate music selections, as well as the names of the participants. In addition, indicate where the audience is to participate and to stand. A complete script is also provided. It may be duplicated and distributed to those with speaking parts.

PRINTS OF PEACE ADVENT ACTIVITIES

In preparation for the pageant, "Prints of Peace," as well as for the celebration of Christ's birth, use these activities to develop the musical and
the visual portions of the program.

DRAW YOUR DREAM OF PEACE

To a child, a world at peace might seem like an unattainable goal.
Yet one way for young people to contribute to a world at peace is to
imagine what such a place would be like. Once conceptualized, a child
can then begin to work toward that goal. The art activity, "Draw Your
Dream of Peace," which forms a basis for the Christmas pageant "Prints
of Peace," provides an opportunity for children to visualize their con-
cepts of peace within themselves as well as in a family, congregation,
school, neighborhood, community, state, nation, and world.

During Advent, explain the project as well as the program and guide
children in Kindergarten through Grade Five as they draw pictures of
their own "prints of peace." These prints will reflect the message of the
"Prince of Peace"—the Babe of Bethlehem who came to be their personal
Savior as well as the Redeemer of the world.

Offer each child a full sheet of construction, copy or drawing paper
as well as colored pencils, crayons, markers or paints and instruct them
to draw a personal dream of peace on one side of the sheet. In addition,
each person may turn over his or her paper and print a word such as
"Jesus" or a symbol such as a cross, heart, or manger on the blank side.
These may be displayed during the closing number. Be sure to include
the name of the artist on each sheet. Collect the papers to use in the pageant. After the program, the drawings may be displayed in the church or
school or at a public location in the community.

LEARN NEW WORDS TO FAMILIAR TUNES

Learn the new words that are provided for the four songs sung by
various classes throughout the program. Then continue the activity by
creating additional lyrics to be sung to the familiar tunes.

"ALL I WANT FOR CHRISTMAS" *(Grades Two and Three)*
All I want for Christmas is my own TV, my own TV, my own TV.
(Spoken words: With remote!)
All I want for Christmas is my own TV, so I can have a Merry Christmas!

All I want for Christmas is my own laptop, my own laptop, my own laptop.
(Spoken words: And a printer!)

All I want for Christmas is my own laptop, so I can have a Merry Christmas!

All I want for Christmas is my own ten-speed, my own ten-speed, my own ten-speed.
(Spoken words: And a helmet!)
All I want for Christmas is my own ten-speed, so I can have a Merry Christmas!

"IF YOU'RE HAPPY AND YOU KNOW IT" *(Kindergarten and Grade One)*
I have a dream of peace, it looks like this.
I have a dream of peace, it looks like this.
I have a dream of peace, I have a dream of peace, I have a dream of peace, it looks like this.

We want to share our dreams with everyone.
We want to share our dreams with everyone.
We want to share our dreams, we want to share our dreams, we want to share our dreams with everyone.

God sent His dream for us, the Prince of Peace.
God sent His dream for us, the Prince of Peace.
God sent His dream for us, God sent His dream for us, God sent His dream for us, the Prince of Peace.

"JINGLE BELLS" *(Grades Four and Five)*
Bowling balls, roller blades, tennis racquets too!
Downhill skis and entrance fees, good stuff for me and you!
Camping gear, hiking boots, scuba tanks and masks,
Board games for the rainy days, and all we do is ask!
And ask—and ask—and ask—and ask!!!

"JOY TO THE WORLD" *(All)*
Peace in the world! We'll do our part
To do what Jesus taught.
We'll collect food for the hungry,
Find shelter for the homeless,
Spread peace to everyone,
Spread peace to everyone,
Spread peace, spread peace to everyone.

PRINTS OF PEACE Bulletin/Program Format

NAME OF CHURCH, DATE

WELCOME
PRAYER

OPENING CAROL: "It Came upon the Midnight Clear"

PROGRAM
CAST *(in order of appearance):* Mom, Grandma, Dad, Older Child, Middle
Child, Younger Child

Scene 1: As the program begins, Dad and Mom prepare to leave for a
Christmas shopping trip while Grandma remains to baby-sit the
children who are sitting quietly, seemingly absorbed in the Christmas
catalogs.

Scene 2: Middle Child shares Christmas wish list.
Music: "All I Want for Christmas"—Grades Two and Three with Middle
Child

Scene 3: Older Child declares Christmas gift ideas.
Music: "Jingle Bells"—Grades Four and Five with Older Child

Scene 4: Younger Child draws a "Print of Peace."
Music: "I Have a Dream of Peace"—Kindergarten and Grade One with
Younger Child

Scene 5: Grandma and Younger Child share "Prints of Peace" idea with
Middle and Older Children.

Scene 6: Parents return home and support "Prints of Peace" project.
Music: "Peace in the World"—All

CLOSING CAROL: "Hark! the Herald Angels Sing"

ACKNOWLEDGEMENTS (Names)

PRINTS OF PEACE (Script)

Scene 1

As the program begins, Dad and Mom prepare to leave for a Christmas shopping trip while Grandma remains to baby-sit. The children are sitting quietly, seemingly absorbed in the Christmas catalogs.

MOM: Thanks so much for watching the kids for us, Grandma! We're getting our Christmas shopping started early this year! Dear, please bring those sale ads with you!

DAD: Okay, okay. I just hope that some year my Thanksgiving meal will fully settle before we have to begin the Christmas rush! *(Picks up the newspaper advertisements.)*

GRANDMA: At least you two don't spoil these children by giving them everything they want. Just look at these sweet little souls. You wouldn't even know the holiday frenzy is beginning. Kids, come say good-bye to your folks before they head out to go Christmas shopping!

(At the word "shopping" all three children seem to "snap to attention" and rush to their parents with catalogs in hand.)

CHILDREN *(at the same time):* Mom! Dad! Buy me this! I want one of these! Get me this, and this, and this. *(Turning pages frantically.)* Look, look! One just like this . . . please!!!

DAD: Sorry, Mom, gotta get going! The mall sounds like a retreat compared to this!

(Parents disengage from their suddenly frenzied family as quickly as possible, leaving a horrified grandmother alone with out-of-control children. The siblings begin to struggle over who has what catalog. The Younger Child loses possession of a catalog and moves, defeated, to sit and color.)

Scene 2

Middle Child shares Christmas wish list.

MIDDLE CHILD: Hey! That's the catalog I had before. I need that one back. There's a special model in there I need to write down on my wish list! *(He or she struggles with the Older Child who holds the book out of reach while the Middle Child tries to grab it back.)* Grandma! Help!

Grandma: Here, here, let's stop this craziness. Christmas shouldn't make us fight with one another. Christmas is a time of peace. Maybe you just need to sit down and show me what you'd like to have this Christmas.

Middle Child: Yeah! Let me show you my wish list, Grandma! You see, I've been cutting out pictures of all the things I really want this Christmas. I know I'd be the happiest kid alive, if only I could find this stuff underneath our tree this Christmas—with *MY* name on all of the packages! *(Music begins.)*

(As the Middle Child unfurls the "wish list," children in Grades Two and Three enter and begin to sing with the Middle Child new words to the song "All I Want for Christmas.")

All I want for Christmas is my own TV, my own TV, my own TV. *(Spoken words: With remote!)*
All I want for Christmas is my own TV, so I can have a Merry Christmas!

All I want for Christmas is my own laptop, my own laptop, my own laptop. *(Spoken words: And a printer!)*
All I want for Christmas is my own laptop, so I can have a Merry Christmas!

All I want for Christmas is my own ten-speed, my own ten-speed, my own ten-speed. *(Spoken words: And a helmet!)*
All I want for Christmas is my own ten-speed, so I can have a Merry Christmas!

(The song can be continued with additional "All I wants . . ." as long as desired. As the music fades and Grades Two and Three leave, the Middle Child looks longingly at the pictures on the wish list.)

Scene 3

Older Child declares Christmas gift ideas.

Older Child: What a selfish picture of Christmas! You want everything for yourself. *(Mockingly.)* "My own, my own, my own!" Christmas shouldn't be about just getting stuff for ourselves.

Grandma : Right! I'm so proud of you!

Older Child: Yeah, we should think about getting stuff *ALL* of us can use! Right, Grandma?

GRANDMA: *(pride beginning to fade):* Well . . .

OLDER CHILD: See, I have a perfect picture of Christmas in my head! We should all be gathered around the tree on Christmas morning . . . *(Group of children in Grades Four and Five begin to enter.)* And there should be tons of presents piled under the tree! And every present should be something that we can all enjoy. You know . . . things like . . . *(Turns pages of the catalog as the music begins. Older Child and Grades Four and Five Chorus sing new words to the tune of "Jingle Bells.")*

Bowling balls, roller blades, tennis racquets too!
Downhill skis and entrance fees, good stuff for me and you!
Camping gear, hiking boots, scuba tanks and masks,
Board games for the rainy days, and all we do is ask!
And ask—and ask—and ask—and ask!!!

(Older Child and Chorus continue to repeat the last line as a marching cadence, until Grades Four and Five leave.)

Scene 4

Younger Child draws a print of peace.

GRANDMA: *(shaking her head):* Somewhere along the line, we must have failed you.

(Middle Child and Older Children look at Grandma, then each other, and shrug their shoulders. The Middle Child grabs the catalog while the Older Child isn't protecting it. A chase ensues and they run offstage, leaving Grandma alone with the Younger Child who has been taking all of this in while coloring a picture.)

GRANDMA: At least one of you seems to have settled down! *(Seemingly talking to herself.)* Oh, my! At this rate, how will we last all the weeks until Christmas? And what kind of Christmas will it be? Isn't Christmas suppose to inspire us to live in peace? There should be a catalog for the Prince of Peace!

YOUNGER CHILD: I have some prints of peace I could give you, Grandma. Is that what you'd like for Christmas?

GRANDMA: You have what?

YOUNGER CHILD: Some prints of peace. I just drew some. Here's my hand-print that I turned into a dove. In Sunday School we learned that a dove is a symbol of peace, and I can make a dove out of my handprint.

See! Doesn't that make this the prints of peace you would like to buy?

GRANDMA: *(hugging the small child):* Oh, sweet child! Not prints like handprints, but prince like someone who will become king. Jesus is our Prince of Peace, and we don't need to buy Him. Christmas celebrates that God sent Jesus, the Prince of Peace, as a free gift to every heart who will receive Him.

YOUNGER CHILD: Oh, then you don't want my picture?

GRANDMA: Of course I do! It's the best Christmas present I can think of! We should make a catalog of pictures just like this so everyone can see what Christmas is really about!

YOUNGER CHILD: That would be cool! I'll help! If we all draw our dream of peace, then maybe more people would look for God's free Gift at Christmas!

(Music begins and Chorus of Kindergarten and First Graders enters. Younger Child sings the first line of the new words to the tune "If You're Happy and You Know It"; then one by one the others join in and add their pictures of their dreams of peace.)

YOUNGER CHILD: I have a dream of peace, it looks like this. *(Holds up picture.)*

ONE CHILD: I have a dream of peace, it looks like this. *(Holds up picture.)*

ADDITIONAL CHILDREN *(in turn):* I have a dream of peace, I have a dream of peace, I have a dream of peace it looks like this. *(Hold up pictures.)*

ALL CHILDREN: We want to share our dreams with everyone. *(All hold up pictures together.)*

We want to share our dreams with everyone.

We want to share our dreams, we want to share our dreams, we want to share our dreams with everyone.

God sent His dream for us, the Prince of Peace.

God sent His dream for us, the Prince of Peace.

God sent His dream for us, God sent His dream for us, God sent His dream for us, the Prince of Peace.

(Kindergarten and Grade One Chorus leaves as the music fades leaving only Grandma and the Younger Child on stage. They embrace.)

Scene 5

Grandma and Younger Child share "Prints of Peace" idea with Middle and Older Children.

GRANDMA: What a wonderful idea! If we could get people to draw their dreams of peace while they wait for Christmas, maybe more hearts would be ready to receive the Prince of Peace this year!

(Middle and Older Children return still quarreling about the catalogs. Grandma interrupts.)

GRANDMA: Here, let me see what you find so fascinating in these books. *(She snatches the catalogs away from both of them.)*
OLDER CHILD: Hey, Grandma, that's not fair. Give them back!
GRANDMA: Okay, I will—if you can tell me one simple thing.
OLDER AND MIDDLE CHILDREN: What?
GRANDMA: Name one thing that you received for Christmas last year.

(Silence.)

GRANDMA: Okay, what about the year before that?
OLDER AND MIDDLE CHILDREN: Uhhh. . . .
GRANDMA: Let me tell you something very important. In a few weeks, all these pictures of "things" will become distant memories too. This Christmas let's make a memory that won't fade, what do you say?
OLDER AND MIDDLE CHILDREN: What's that?
GRANDMA *(to Younger Child):* You tell them our idea.
YOUNGER CHILD Grandma and I want to help people make prints of peace.
OLDER AND MIDDLE CHILDREN: What?
GRANDMA: It's a play on words, get it? If we could help people to draw a picture or make a print of one way that they can help bring peace to the world, then maybe this Christmas we will be closer to realizing God's dream for this world. Would you like to be a part of something that could make a world of difference?
YOUNGER CHILD: Yes!
OLDER AND MIDDLE CHILDREN: What would we have to do?
GRANDMA: Well, let's start by creating our own prints of peace. What can *YOU* do to picture a world where people live God's dream of peace?
MIDDLE CHILD: I guess I'd draw a world where brothers and sisters share! *(Takes a catalog from Grandma and hands it to the Older Child.)*

OLDER CHILD (*speaking to Younger Child*): Hey, may I please use some of your markers and paper? I'd like to draw a dream of peace showing that everyone has a friend.

GRANDMA: If we could get your friends to join us, maybe we could get some sponsors to let us create a display at the mall.

MIDDLE CHILD: Maybe we could set up a booth at the mall, and children— or anyone—could draw their dreams to add to our collection!

OLDER AND YOUNGER CHILD: Cool! (*All get paper and crayons or markers and get to work.*)

Scene 6

Parents return home and support "Prints of Peace" project. Parents enter cautiously and are surprised to find such calm.

MOM AND DAD: Wow!

DAD: What a different picture this is than when we left.

MOM: What happened?

YOUNGER CHILD: It's easy, Mom. We found the best Christmas gift—The Prints of Peace!

(*All hold up their drawings. Music for "Joy to the World" begins as all of the Children's Choruses reenter. Participants sing the alternate words provided as a closing number.*)

ALL: Peace in the world! We'll do our part
To do what Jesus taught.
We'll collect food for the hungry,
Find shelter for the homeless,
Spread peace to everyone, Spread peace to everyone,
Spread peace, spread peace to everyone.

(*Continue singing new words for lines three and four as long as desired. Conclude the program with a Benediction or a Closing Prayer.*)

THE MENAGERIE AT THE MANGER

THEME: Christmas is a time to experience God's message with all of our senses.

SUMMARY: The animals that could have been with baby Jesus and His family on the first Christmas Day represent the five senses, challenging us to have a "sense-able" Christmas. Scripture lessons, narration, actions, and original lyrics trace five themes as the donkey invites us to hear love, the dog to smell hope, the dove to taste peace, the cow to touch joy, and the sheep to see light. This fresh approach to the familiar story appeals to both children and adults with its down-to-earth message from the menagerie at the manger.

SUGGESTIONS: "The Menagerie at the Manger" is a program, staged in a pageant or a worship setting, that can be presented simply or elaborately with many or few participants. It is suggested that each class, representing different ages and grades of children, have a specific part in the preparation and the presentation of this program. For example,

Kindergarten and Grade One, "Hear Love": The Donkey, Sound
   Symphony

Grade Two: "Smell Hope": The Dog, Clown and Puppet Skit

Grade Three: "Taste Peace": The Dove, Creative Movement

Grade Four: "Touch Joy": The Cow, "Name That Touch" Game Show

Grade Five: "See Light": The Lamb, "Children's Message." Animal
   Construction, Candlelighters, Gift Box Decoration, Scripture Readers,
   Speakers

If younger children, such as nursery and preschool boys and girls are included in the program, they may open the gift boxes and place the animal figures around the manger, sing in a cherub choir, and participate in the closing nativity scene.

Speaking parts may be broken down further to allow for more than one participant per reading. For example, the Scripture could be shared responsively between two readers or verses may be assigned to members of a class. The "Speaker" sections could have different people read each paragraph. One costumed character per section should be designated to light one of the four Advent candles, as well as the Christ candle at the conclusion of each scene.

Of course, the scenes should take place where they can be seen from all parts of the audience. The participants may simply strike a pose in the center of the chancel area or on a raised platform. The program could also take place on a stage in a social hall. Actors should be costumed appropriately to suggest their parts, adding props that help project the image of each character.

Music might range from instrumental or vocal solo performances to class, choir, group, or congregational singing. Additional or alternate carols may be substituted for those suggested; however, the original song "Light the Advent/Christmas Candles," sung to the tune "Go, Tell It on the Mountain" should be used throughout the program.

Advent activities involve each class in preparation for their part of the pageant. An outline for a printed bulletin or program is offered; however, it must be adapted to include additional or alternate music selections, as well as the names of the participants. In addition, indicate where the congregation is to participate and to stand. A complete script is also provided. It may be duplicated and distributed to those with speaking parts. Suggestions for Cast/Personnel, Costumes, and Props are provided.

CAST: Angel (candlelighter, nativity scene), Children's Choir *(optional)*, Clown, Conductor, Dogs—Grade Two, Gift Box Openers (5), Joseph (candlelighter, nativity scene), Mary (candlelighter, nativity scene), Mimes—Grade Three, "Name That Touch" Participants—Grade Four, Pastor/Worship Leader, Scripture Readers, Shepherd (candlelighter, nativity scene), Shepherd (dog scene), Speakers, Sound Symphony—Kindergarten and Grade One, Wise Man (candlelighter, nativity scene)
PERSONNEL: Accompanist, Children's Choir Director, Lighting Technician, Pageant Director, Sound Coordinator

COSTUMES: Angel, Clown, Conductor, Dogs, Joseph, Mary, Shepherd (2), Wise man

PROPS: Advent wreath with four purple candles; animal figures: cow, dog, donkey, dove, lamb; baby doll; baton; candles; chairs (3); Christ candle; gift boxes (5); manger; matches. Music: anthems "Light the Advent/Christmas Candles," "Sweet Little Jesus Boy," "The Friendly Beasts." Carols. Recording: "The Dance of the Sugar Plum Fairy" from the *Nutcracker Suite*; music stand; posters/props of food; props for Clown; table (sound symphony), touch boxes, toys (sound symphony)

EQUIPMENT: keyboard, organ or piano; lighting equipment; microphones; sound system

THE MENAGERIE AT THE MANGER ADVENT ACTIVITIES

In anticipation of the pageant, "The Menagerie at the Manger," use the activities suggested to prepare each class for their specific part in the program.

Kindergarten/Grade One—Sound Symphony
Kindergarten and Grade One children create a "Sound Symphony" as their special part of the Christmas program. In preparation for the event, invite each participant to bring a toy that makes noise. To practice for the pageant, place the toys on a table and assemble the children behind it. A "Conductor" walks to a music stand placed in front of the table, picks up a baton, and begins to "direct" the "orchestra." At the Conductor's signal, all participants pick up their "instruments"—one toy per person—and wait for the Conductor's cue to play. Each person, in turn, begins to make the "music" by turning on the power button on the toy or by providing the motion to make the desired sound. At first each sound is distinct; but as more toys and objects are "performed," the clatter increases. Finally, the Conductor signals the players to stop. Everyone takes a bow and remains in place to listen to the Speaker.

Grade Two—Dog Body Puppets or Costumes
Canine costumes for the Second Graders may be created by combining black, brown, tan, and white fleece pants and shirts, as well as headbands with dog ears and rubber animal noses. They may also be developed by having each child construct a body puppet to wear in the program.

Materials: brown paper grocery bags, construction paper, glue, markers, plastic bags, rubber bands (*medium, two per puppet*), scissors, stapler, staples, yarn

Method: Create dog costumes by turning paper and plastic bags into body puppets. For each puppet, start with a full-size brown paper grocery bag. The bottom flap of it will become the puppet's head, and the remainder of the bag will be the body. Glue a full sheet of construction paper to the body portion of the bag. Make a face on the flap. Decorate the character with markers and additional construction paper. Make a neck strap by cutting a 30" piece of yarn. Staple the center of the yarn to the middle of the top of the bag. For arms, cut two 18" x 2" strips of plastic bag. Tie a rubber band to the end of each piece of plastic. Staple the other end of each arm strip to the paper bag, just below the flap.

To wear and work the puppet, tie the yarn around the child's neck, and slip the rubber bands over the wrists. The puppeteer's motions and movements manipulate the puppet.

Grade Three—Creative Movement

Children in Grade Three mime their dreams of the tastes of the season. In preparation, they may make posters or props to illustrate these items. As music for the "Dance of the Sugar Plum Fairy" from the *Nutcracker Suite* starts, Third Graders enter and interpret the process of dreaming about the tastes of the season. A few children pretend to be "tucked in their beds" asleep. The other participants interpret the music as they move around those who "sleep" and display their posters and props. At the close of the music, the dancers exit and the sleeping ones awake, stand, and exclaim "I'm starving! Let's eat!" All exit.

Grade Four—Touch Boxes

Children in Grade Four explore the sense of "touch" as their unique contribution to the pageant. To create the "Touch Boxes," cover at least three shoe boxes, or cartons of any size, with wrapping paper. Cut an opening, large enough for a hand to reach inside the box, at one end of each container. Place one item associated with a touch of Christmas inside each box. Articles may include an evergreen branch, a figure from a nativity scene, or an unbreakable ornament.

Since the Fourth Graders participate in a "Name That Touch" game show format during the pageant, practice the potential interaction that will take place with the contestants who will be selected from the audience.

Grade Five and Older Youth—Animal Figures, Candlelighters, Gift Boxes, Scripture Readers and Speakers

Prior to the program, Students in Grade Five as well as any other older youth, should practice parts in connection with their roles as candlelighters, Scripture readers, and speakers.

In addition, they may also construct the animal figures and decorate five boxes to hold the shapes. Symbols representing the cow, dog, donkey, dove, and lamb may be made from cardboard, foam core or plywood. Photocopy simple outlines onto transparencies to project on whatever material will be used for the animals. Fasten the background material to the wall and position an overhead projector to get the desired animal size. Trace the outline with pencil or marker. Cut out the animals and place them on the floor or on a table to paint. Acrylic paint is suitable for almost any surface. Paint with large brushes or sponges. For realistic textures, add fake fur, stuffing and other enhancements. Draw or attach other details.

Cover the corresponding cartons with paint or paper.

All—Music: Teach the participants the music for the two anthems as well as for the theme song, "Light the Advent/Christmas Candles." Anthems: "Sweet Little Jesus Boy," "The Friendly Beasts" Theme Carol: "Light the Advent Candles" *(Tune: "Go, Tell It on the Mountain." See script for words.)*

THE MENAGERIE AT THE MANGER Bulletin/Program Format

PRELUDE

PROCESSIONAL HYMN: "O Come, All Ye Faithful"

CALL TO WORSHIP *(Pastor or Worship Leader reads Part "One" and Audience and Participants respond with phrases marked "All.")*
ONE: God invites us here to celebrate the gift of new life, not only the birth of Jesus, but the rebirth of our faith.
ALL: Although God's presence is beyond our comprehension, we can sense God-with-us in the sights, smells, sounds, tastes, and touches of this season.
ONE: Let the reality of God's love surround us as we worship in the name of Christ, the Holy One of God.

CAROL: "Good Christian Men, Rejoice"

INVOCATION

ANTHEM: "Sweet Little Jesus Boy"

THE CHRISTMAS STORY BEGINS: "HEAR LOVE!" Luke 2:1-5
"Hear Love: the Donkey"
"Sound Symphony"—Kindergarten and Grade One
CAROL: "Light the Advent Candles" *(Verse 1 and Chorus)*
Lighting the first candle

ALL IS NOW READY: "SMELL HOPE!" Luke 2:6, 7
"Smell Hope: the Dog" Clown and Puppet Skit—Grade Two
CAROL: "Light the Advent Candles" *(Verse 2 and Chorus)*
Lighting the second candle

CAROL: "There's a Song in the Air"

THE ANGEL'S ANNOUNCEMENT: "TASTE PEACE!" Luke 2:8-14
"Taste Peace: the Dove" Creative Movement—Grade Three
CAROL: "Light the Advent Candles" *(Verse 3 and Chorus)*
Lighting the third candle

THE STABLE IS CROWDED: "TOUCH JOY!" Luke 2:15-16
"Touch Joy: the Cow" "Name That Touch" Game—Grade Four
Passing the Peace
CAROL: "Light the Advent Candles" *(Verse 4 and Chorus)*
Lighting the fourth candle

THE BABY IS JESUS: "SEE LIGHT!" Luke 2:17-20
"See Light: the Lamb" Children's Message
CAROL: "Light the Christmas Candle" *(Verse 5 and Chorus)*
Lighting the Christ candle

ANTHEM: "The Friendly Beasts"

THE MESSAGE CONTINUES John 1:1-5

CAROL: "Away in a Manger"

CLOSING CHALLENGE *(Congregation passes the light.)*

CAROL: "Joy to the World!"

BENEDICTION

POSTLUDE

THE MENAGERIE AT THE MANGER (Script)

PRELUDE *(Children and youth perform a variety of instrumental and vocal Christmas music.)*

PROCESSIONAL HYMN: "O Come, All Ye Faithful"

(During the Processional Hymn, all participants in the program enter and take their places in designated areas on the stage or in reserved seats in the audience. One child per class, Kindergarten through Grade Five, may carry the manger and the five wrapped gifts and place them in the center of the performance area. As an alternative, the scene may be set in advance.)

CALL TO WORSHIP *(Pastor or Worship Leader reads Part "One" and Audience and Participants respond with phrases marked "All.")*
ONE: God invites us here to celebrate the gift of new life, not only the birth of Jesus, but the rebirth of our faith.
ALL: Although God's presence is beyond our comprehension, we can sense God-with-us in the sights, smells, sounds, tastes, and touches of this season.
ONE: Let the reality of God's love surround us as we worship in the name of Christ, the Holy One of God.

CAROL: "Good Christian Men, Rejoice!"

INVOCATION *(Pastor or Worship Leader offers prayer.)* God of all creation, quicken our weary hearts by Your Holy Spirit. Sensitize us to Your Presence, and give us the power to celebrate with all the host of Heaven the glorious news that Christ is born! Grant us, we pray, a humble faith ready to receive His rebirth in our lives today. Amen.

ANTHEM: "Sweet Little Jesus Boy" *(Children's Choir or Older Class enter or stand and sing and then leave or sit after song.)*

THE CHRISTMAS STORY BEGINS: "HEAR LOVE!" *(Scripture Reader and Speaker(s) enter.)* Scripture: Luke 2:1-5
"Hear Love: the Donkey" "Sound Symphony" *(Kindergarten and Grade One)*

SPEAKER: Can you hear the sound of Christmas love? Does it sound like money clinking in cash registers? Does it sound like battery-powered chimes repeating twenty-five different Christmas carols? Or does it sound like holiday toys? Christmas can be noisy—so noisy that we don't hear God's still small voice. To emphasize this point, I introduce to you a distinguished conductor: the Maestro of Christmas Clatter!

(Kindergarten and First Grade children assemble behind a table filled with a variety of noisy toys. A "Conductor," dressed formally, walks to a music stand, picks up his baton, and begins to "direct" the "orchestra." At the Conductor's signal, all participants pick up their "instruments"—one toy per person—and wait for the Conductor's cue to play. Each person, in turn, begins to make the "music" by turning on the power button on the toy or by providing the motion to make the desired sound. At first each sound is distinct, but as more toys and objects are "performed" the clatter increases. Finally, the Conductor signals the players to stop. Everyone takes a bow and remains in place to listen to the Speaker.)

SPEAKER: At Christmas we need to listen for something more than the usual clatter. We need to hear God's "still, small voice." If we want to hear the sound of Christmas love, we must choose to listen for the voice of God. At the manger of Bethlehem, one animal stands as a reminder to turn our ears toward God.

(One child opens the wrapped package and places the donkey at the manger display.)

SPEAKER: The donkey reminds us to train our ears to listen for the voice of the One we can trust. Just as the tone of father Joseph's reassuring words quieted the little donkey as he was led to Bethlehem, so God's message in Jesus can bring us peace as we travel through life. Our ears must strain to hear—not the noise and problems around us—but the soothing sound of a loving voice. "Do not fear. Follow me. All is well." Are you listening?

CAROL: "Light the Advent Candles" *(Verse 1 and Chorus, tune: "Go, Tell It on the Mountain")*
Verse: The donkey starts our journey, To Bethlehem to hear, The news the people long for, That Christ is drawing near.
Chorus: Light the Advent candles, Let them burn brightly far and near! Sending out their message, That Jesus will soon be here!

LIGHTING THE FIRST CANDLE: *(Youth dressed as Joseph lights the first candle during the singing. Participants exit during the chorus.)*

ALL IS NOW READY: "SMELL HOPE!" *(Scripture Reader and Speaker(s) enter.)* Scripture: Luke 2:6-7

"Smell Hope: the Dog" Clown and Puppet Skit *(Grade Two)*

SPEAKER: Don't you just love the smells of Christmas? Why, we have a special guest to help us "sniff out" these wonderful scents! *(Clown enters and joins Speaker.)* Welcome, Schnozz. I understand that your nose knows smells!

CLOWN *(looks around nervously):* Hello, Folks! Glad to "nose" ya! Please forgive me, but I'm a little nervous. I think something's gotten wind of me!

SPEAKER: We were just discussing the joy of Christmas scents. With your superpowerful nose, Schnozz, tell us what you smell this Christmas.

CLOWN *(takes a big sniff and begins to pull pictures or props from his bag or pockets):* Hmmm . . . let's see. I catch the scent of fragrant pine, spicy cinnamon, fresh-baked bread, steaming hot chocolate, and a big Christmas turkey! *(He pulls out a turkey drumstick.)* But wait . . . I think I smell something else . . . dogs!

(Second Graders appear wearing dog body puppets or costumes. They chase the clown off stage. After the commotion, a Shepherd runs in.)

SHEPHERD: Wait! Wait! Those are my dogs! They have to help me tend the sheep! Come back! *(Shepherd runs after the dogs calling for them; then he stops with an "idea!" He pulls an even larger turkey leg from his pockets or pouch. Suddenly the dogs reappear and happily chase the Shepherd out the way they came in.)*

SPEAKER: The Shepherd's dogs know what it means to catch the scent of something better! That's what we need to do too. To truly enjoy the experience of Christmas, we must try to catch the scent of God's special gift—the gift of hope. Surely when the shepherds came to the manger of Bethlehem, at least one of their faithful canine companions would have followed the scent of new hope in the air.

(One child opens the wrapped package and places the dog at the manger display.)

SPEAKER: The shepherd's faithful dog reminds us to follow the scent of hope this Christmas. Can't you imagine that before the shepherds in the field heard any angel voice, the dog already knew that something was "in the air"? And, when they left for Bethlehem to search for the newborn Babe, don't you think the dog led the way, letting the scent of manger hay guide each step? We, too, must lift our heads and follow the fragrance that leads us to God. The fragrance is hope—hope that rests in the manger hay. Do you catch the scent?

CAROL: "Light the Advent Candles" *(Verse 2 and Chorus)*
Verse: The dog can sense the fragrance, Of hope that's in the air,
  Expectantly awaiting, God's Christmas joy to share.
Chorus: Light the Advent candles, Let them burn brightly far and near,
  Sending out their message, That Jesus will soon be here.

LIGHTING THE SECOND CANDLE: *(Youth dressed as Shepherd lights the
  second candle during the singing. Participants exit during the chorus.)*

CAROL: "There's a Song in the Air" *(optional)*

THE ANGEL'S ANNOUNCEMENT: "TASTE PEACE!" *(Scripture Reader
  and Speaker(s) enter.)* Scripture: Luke 2:8-14
"Taste Peace: the Dove" Creative Movement *(Grade Three)*

SPEAKER: What's your favorite Christmas flavor? Peppermint? Fruitcake?
  Eggnog? There are so many that it's easy to put on extra pounds trying to taste them all! The holidays are a time when visions of sugar
  plums dance through our heads.

(As music for the "Dance of the Sugar Plum Fairy" from the Nutcracker Suite
*starts, Third Graders enter and begin to mime the process of dreaming about the
tastes of the season. A few children pretend to be "tucked in their beds" asleep.
The other participants interpret the music as they represent the variety of foods
about which the children may dream. They should have props or posters as they
move behind and around the heads of those who "sleep." At the close of the
music, the dancers exit and the sleeping ones awake, stand, and exclaim, "I'm
starving! Let's eat!" They exit.)*

SPEAKER: During the holidays we eat so much that we think we'll never
  be hungry again! However, somehow that satisfaction doesn't last. We
  may keep looking for a new taste sensation, but no flavor on earth will
  truly satisfy us forever. You see, humans have a hunger for something
  more than even the greatest Christmas feast can fill. When Jesus was
  born, there might have been a small dove that cooed quietly in that
  Bethlehem stable. The dove symbolizes our being filled with what we
  hunger for most—a sense of peace.

(A child opens the wrapped package and places the dove at the manger display.)

SPEAKER: The dove with the olive branch in its mouth symbolizes the
  Christmas gift that truly satisfies. What we humans hunger for more

than anything else is peace. If we are to taste this satisfying flavor of Christmas, then we must first acknowledge our hunger so that God can send us the gift the angels sang about that first Christmas morning—peace on earth. Are you willing to be filled with the spirit of peace?

CAROL: "Light the Advent Candles" *(Verse 3 and Chorus)*
Verse: The dove within its mouth holds, The olive branch of peace, And everyone who's hungry, Is invited to God's feast.
Chorus: Light the Advent candles, Let them burn brightly far and near, Sending out their message, That Jesus will soon be here.

LIGHTING THE THIRD CANDLE *(Youth dressed as Angel lights the third candle during the singing. Participants exit during the chorus.)*

THE STABLE IS CROWDED: "TOUCH JOY!" *(Scripture Reader and Speaker(s) enter.)* Scripture: Luke 2:15-16
"Touch Joy: the Cow" "Name That Touch" Game *(Grade Four)*

SPEAKER: What do your fingertips like best about Christmas—the velvety bows on beautiful green wreaths or the prickly pine needles? There are many "touches" of Christmas, aren't there? The soft fur of a new teddy bear that you receive as a gift probably feels better than the jostling and bumping of the Christmas crowd when you do last-minute shopping.

Our Fourth Graders have prepared a Christmas game show for you to experience called, "Name That Touch!" Now our Fourth Grade Hosts will "Come on down!" and pick three unsuspecting contestants to help us play the game!

(Fourth Graders enter. Three are carrying "Touch Boxes." Three youth go into the audience to select and escort three "Contestants" to the front where the others have arranged a chair and a touch box for each player. The students hold the touch boxes and give instructions to each participant to reach in, feel the item, and whisper one guess about the contents to the escort.)

EMCEE: Okay, participants! Name that touch!
Contestant Number One, what Christmas touch do you recognize?
Contestant Number Two . . . ? Contestant Number Three . . . ?

(Congratulate the winners and tell them that they have won a hug from the students. Then tell the "Contestants" who were wrong that they win the

"consolation prize"—a hug from the students. Thank everyone with applause and dismiss the Contestants to their seats. Fourth graders sit on and around the chairs until it is time to lead the congregation in "Passing the Peace.")

SPEAKER: There must have been many different textures to remind Joseph and Mary of the first Christmas morning: the fur of the animals crowding the stable; the cold, raw air that came in with the shepherds; the scratchy hay of the Christ Child's crib; and the soft cloths swaddling the sweet skin of their newborn Son. Among the animals that crowded the stable, there was one that stood to comfort the holy family with the warmth of her presence—the cow.

(A child opens the wrapped package and places the cow at the manger display.)

SPEAKER: The cow reminds us of the joyous warmth of that first Christmas morning. Legend says that the cow gave up her hay-filled manger for the Christ Child's first bed, then stood near the baby to warm Him with her breath. Jesus' world may have been cold and scratchy—like ours often is—but those around Him, His parents and the animals too, worked together to bring warmth and gentleness to life.

     Do you know someone who needs a touch of Christmas joy—like a hug or an "I-love-you" squeeze of the hand? Will you stand near to warm them?

PASSING THE PEACE *(Fourth Graders lead the congregation in greeting one another, shaking hands and exchanging words of peace.)*

CAROL: "Light the Advent Candles" *(Verse 4 and Chorus)*
Verse: The cow provides her warmth for, The baby from above, The hay holds baby Jesus, Who touches hearts with love.
Chorus: Light the Advent candles, Let them burn brightly far and near, Sending out their message, That Jesus will soon be here.

LIGHTING THE FOURTH CANDLE *(Youth dressed as Mary lights the fourth candle during the singing. Participants exit during the chorus, removing the chairs if necessary.)*

THE BABY IS JESUS: "SEE LIGHT!" *(Scripture Reader and Speaker(s) enter.)* Scripture: Luke 2:17-20
"See Light: the Lamb"

CHILDREN'S MESSAGE *(Speaker, possibly the Pastor, enters and invites all children to come forward for the Children's Message.)*

Do you enjoy the lights of Christmas? Everywhere we look we see displays blinking green and red, trees outlined in white, or candles flickering a golden glow in windows. The lights of Christmas brighten our holidays only to the extent that we are able to see more clearly the true meaning of the season. When Christ was born at Christmas, Jesus brought God's light to earth in a special way. It is possible that the light of that love was offered first to those friendly beasts that welcomed Him on Christmas Day, for Jesus himself is known as the Lamb of God.

(A child opens the wrapped package and places the lamb at the manger display.)

SPEAKER: The wooly lamb at the manger reminds us to open our eyes to see the light—Jesus is born, the Savior of the world. Are you ready to behold the Lamb of God?

CAROL: "Light the Christmas Candle" *(Verse 5 and Chorus)*
Verse: The sheep kneels at the manger, And bows his horns so curled, To see the Lamb of God, Who's the Savior of the world.
Chorus: Light the Christmas candle, Let it burn brightly far and near, Sending out the message, That Jesus Christ is here.

LIGHTING THE CHRIST CANDLE *(Youth dressed as Wise man lights the Christ candle during the singing. Participants leave during the chorus.)*

ANTHEM: "The Friendly Beasts" *(Children's Choir or Older Class enter or stand and sing then exit or sit after song.)*

THE MESSAGE CONTINUES *(Scripture Reader and Speaker enter.)*
Scripture: John 1:1-5

SPEAKER: Christ is born! The Light of the World has come. All the darkness that exists cannot extinguish that light. And now we are asked to become messengers—to take the news of God's light-come-to-earth to every place where we live, and work, and visit. It isn't difficult when Jesus lives within us. All of our senses come alive, and the light of His love shines out through us to everyone we meet.

CAROL: "Away in a Manger"

(Create a nativity scene as a focal point during the singing of the carol. The five Candlelighters, dressed in costumes to represent Joseph, Mary, Shepherd, Angel, and Wise man gather around the manger to form the scene. Mary carries a baby or a doll and places the "Christ Child" in the creche. All program participants may be invited to join in the closing setting.)

SPEAKER: Christ is born! We have heard the story again. Now we must become the story. We must go and tell. Are you ready to begin?

CAROL: "Joy to the World!"

(As the carol begins, the worship leader lights a candle from the Christ candle, and in turn lights the candles of the ushers, who then take the light to the first person in each pew. Each person, in turn, "passes the light" to his or her neighbor.)

BENEDICTION

POSTLUDE

(Participants recess during Postlude.)